The Complete ASTB Study Guide

ASTB PRACTICE TESTS AND PREPARATION GUIDE
FOR THE ASTB EXAM

John Mackey

This book is dedicated to the brave men and women who serve the United States armed forces. Without your vigilance we wouldn't have the freedom and liberty we have today.

Contents

ASTB INTRODUCTION 1

    Making the Most of Your ASTB Study Guide 1

    ASTB Sections 2

    ASTB Scoring 3

    ASTB FAQs 4

MATH SKILLS TEST (MST) 7

    MST Purpose 7

    MST Contents 8

    MST Preparation 15

    MST Practice Test 16

    MST Answer Key 20

READING COMPREHENSION TEST (RCT) 21

    RCT Purpose 21

    RCT Contents 22

    RCT Preparation 29

    RCT Practice Test 30

    RCT Answer Key 37

AVIATION AND NAUTICAL INFORMATION TEST (ANIT) 39

    ANIT Purpose 39

    ANIT Contents 40

    ANIT Preparation 48

    ANIT Practice Test 49

ANIT Answer Key 53

MECHANICAL COMPREHENSION TEST (MCT) 55

MCT Purpose 55

MCT Contents..56

MCT Preparation..73

MCT Practice Test 74

MCT Answer Key 78

ASTB CONCLUSION...79

USEFUL EXTERNAL ASTB RESOURCES...81

ASTB Introduction

Becoming a flight officer in the Navy, Marine Corps, or Coast Guard is one of the most desirable careers in the entire military. It is also one of the most competitive. The ASTB-E, or Aviation Selection Test Battery to give it its full name, is the series of tests used to determine whether a candidate shows aptitude for flight training and represents a good prospect for success at later stages of the training program.

The ASTB-E is the most recent and up to date version of the test, with a range of adaptations and upgrades from previous versions of the ASTB. However, for the sake of brevity, this book will refer to the test as the ASTB from this point forward. At all times, this is referring to the ASTB-E however, and the information is the most up to date possible for the latest version of the Test Battery.

The military uses a testing platform called Automated Pilot Examination, commonly abbreviated as APEX. The ASTB is tested through this platform only, meaning that your test will be in an electronic format.

Making the Most of Your ASTB Study Guide

Each section of this ASTB study guide consists of several sections: Purpose, Contents, Preparation, Practice Test, and Practice Test Answer Key.

The Purpose section of each chapter explains the reason why the ASTB features this particular test. It's been proven that understanding the purpose and reason behind a test increases one's motivation to study for it. The Purpose section is therefore a proven way of increasing your motivation for a particular section, as well as explaining to you how it may be useful to your future Aviation career.

The Contents section breaks down the type of material you are likely to encounter during that portion of the ASTB. All the information in this guide has been taken from test takers reporting the type of content they faced. This ensures that all the material you cover stands a good chance of being found on the ASTB.

The Preparation section gives tips for studying and ways of processing the information. These sections have been written with different learning styles in mind, and they are intended to be useful for those seeking optimum strategies to absorb and retain the information.

The Practice Test section features a range of questions to test your knowledge and application of the chapter's content.

The Practice Test Answer Key allows you to quickly and easily check your answers for each section of the ASTB practice test. This is vital to identify areas that are understood well, and those which require additional study and practice.

ASTB Sections

The ASTB consists of seven sections. Below are the full names for each section, the abbreviations by which they are commonly known, and the most essential information about each section.

1. Math Skills Test (MST)

Consists of between 20 and 30 multiple choice questions. This is a computer adaptive section, meaning the exact number and nature of the test questions you receive will vary depending upon your previous answers.

2. Reading Comprehension Test (RCT)

Between 20 and 30 multiple choice questions, as determined by the computer adaptive testing system. Each question consists of a passage of text and four possible answers. Only one answer is definitely true based on the text passage given, although all may seem related or initially plausible.

3. Mechanical Comprehension Test (MCT)

Between 20 and 30 multiple choice questions, as determined by the computer adaptive system. Each question tests either a practical or theoretical aspect of mechanics and physics, ranging from abstract concepts (such as Newton's Laws) to applied ideas (such as the stages of an engine's operation).

4. Aviation and Nautical Information Test (ANIT)

Between 20 and 30 multiple choice questions relating to the practical aspects of flight, such as how an airport operates, the history of the Navy, and information relating to

Naval aircraft and ship naming conventions. The number of questions is determined by the computer adaptive system.

5. Naval Aviation Trait Facet Inventory (NATFI)

A type of personality test in which you are given a pair of statements and asked to choose between them. This section cannot be studied for. You should answer honestly rather than trying to "game the system," as it is designed to identify any deceptive answers via the way the questions are worded. This is intended to determine whether you have the personality traits that correlate with success in Naval Aviation training.

6. Performance Based Measures Battery (PBM)

This is the most hands-on, practical portion of the ASTB. It involves the use of an imitation throttle, joystick, and headset. It does not test actual flying ability, rather, it tests your ability to multitask, your manual dexterity, and your ability to process information while filtering out distractions.

7. Biographical Inventory with Response Validation (BI-RV)

This section of the ASTB can be completed at a different time than your main test. It basically checks your personal background, including any aviation experience you've had. This can be taken via any computer connected to the internet. It is generally suggested to take this portion of the ASTB before taking the other sections.

ASTB Scoring

The ASTB score you receive will depend upon which sections of the test you take and your purpose for taking the test.

If you are in the Navy and attempting to enter Officer Candidate School, then you will receive a score based on the first three sections of the test only – the MST, RCT and MCT. This score will be your Officer Aptitude Rating, or OAR. The score range you can receive for the OAR portion of the ASTB is between 20 and 80. The minimum OAR score needed for consideration by Navy Officer Candidate School is 35.

If you complete the full ASTB then you will receive three more scores. These are the AQR (Academic Qualifications Rating), the PFAR (Pilot Flight Aptitude Rating), and the FOFAR (Flight Officer Aptitude Rating).

The AQR, PFAR, and FOFAR are scored between 1 and 9 with a mean score of 5. The minimum scores needed on the AQR, PFAR, and FOFAR are as follows:

Student Naval Aviators (SNAs) are required to score at least a 4 on the AQR and a 5 on the PFAR.

Student Naval Flight Officers (SNFOs) are required to score at least a 4 on the AQR and a 5 on the FOFAR.

Marine Pilots and Marine Flight Officers are required to score at least a 4 on the AQR and a 6 on the FOFAR.

It should be emphasized that the above scores are the minimum. Your scores will be directly compared against the other candidates applying for Aviation training. Therefore, do not aim to hit the minimum. Your objective should be to achieve the highest score possible on each and every section of the test. This approach gives you the best chance of progressing to further Aviation training stages, and also of having a successful future Aviation career.

ASTB FAQs

What is the overall purpose of the ASTB?

The main purpose of the ASTB is to predict whether test takers have the right mix of knowledge, skill, and personality to succeed at later stages of Aviation training. The cost of those not completing later stages of training is high, so the Navy tries to filter out those who are unlikely to succeed in advance, thus saving resources.

How long does the ASTB take?

There is no single test time for the ASTB, as the computer adaptive nature of the test means that no two test takers will see exactly the same test. However, the BI-IV section takes between 45 minutes to 2 hours. For this reason, it is advised that test takers complete this section at home rather than completing it on the day of their ASTB. The remainder of the ASTB takes between 120 and 195 minutes on average. Those who complete only the OAR portion of the ASTB (MST, RCT, and MCT) take between 90 and 120 minutes on average.

Where can I take the ASTB?

The most common locations to take the ASTB include:

- NROTC units at colleges (check with your local college)
- Naval Officer Recruiting Stations
- OSOs (Marine Corps Officer Selection Offices)
- Military Institutes

Which languages can I take the ASTB in?

The ASTB can be taken only in English.

Can I use a calculator on the ASTB?

No, although formulas are provided along with paper for carrying out calculations.

What can I bring with me on the day of the ASTB test?

Candidates must bring photo I.D and proof of Social Security number. For photo I.D, it is suggested that candidates bring their driver's license, military I.D card, or passport.

There is no need to bring pencils and paper as these are provided.

Electronic devices and personal belongings will not be allowed into the testing room, but may be left with test officials or kept in your car.

How do I know which sections of the ASTB to take?

Your recruiting program will advise whether you should take the entire ASTB or just the OAR portion.

What is CAT?

CAT stands for Computer Adaptive Test and is the system used on the ASTB. It means that the type and difficulty of question you are shown will depend upon your prior performance. The exact methods used by the CAT is a closely guarded secret and is not publicly stated.

How do I get my ASTB Scores?

If you take the ASTB or OAR using the APEX computer system, then you will receive scores immediately upon completion of the seven test sections.

If you take the paper version of the OAR, then you can contact via phone at (850) 452-2379 to get an official score letter. You can also request an official score letter via email by contacting usn.pensacola.navmedoptractrpns.list.nmotc-astb@mail.mil. You have to include your full name and final four digits of your Social Security number when requesting an official score letter. If you want to receive your official score by email, you can only get it sent to an email address ending in .mil, .gov, or .edu.

If I have taken the ASTB multiple times, which score counts?

Your most recent score on the ASTB replaces all previous scores, even if the older scores were higher. All record of them will be destroyed and they won't be considered. It is therefore vital to be sure you can get a better score if you decide to retake the ASTB.

Who should I contact about the ASTB?

If you have further questions about the ASTB you should contact the NMOTC Operational Psychology Department via telephone at (850) 452-2379.

You can also email usn.pensacola.navmedoptractrpns.list.nmotc-astb@mail.mil with any questions you have.

Math Skills Test (MST)

MST Purpose

The Math Skills Test of the ASTB is intended to assess your understanding and application of mathematical concepts relevant to your future Navy career. This includes the building blocks of math, such as the order of operations, as well as more applied examples, such as mathematical logic problems.

Similar to the RCT portion of the ASTB, the MST is somewhat removed from the realities of your future, day-to-day life in the Navy. It is unlikely you will ever be presented with a list of equations and asked to solve them. However, your ability to think mathematically and logically will indeed come in useful over the course of your career. For example, if you have limited resources and a mission objective requiring the careful use of these resources, being able to apply and distribute them in a rational way will be essential to achieving your objectives.

The ability to comprehend and apply mathematical concepts is also a predictor of general intelligence, something the Navy is very much testing for with the ASTB. It is unlikely that the MST will cover any aspect of math that is entirely new or unfamiliar to you. However, for many people, it may have been a number of years since the topics have been covered. This section should therefore provide a useful refresher of key mathematical ideas and how to apply them.

MST Contents

Order Of Operations

One of the fundamentals of success in math is having familiarity with and experience using the "order of operations." This is the sequence in which mathematical problems must be solved. The order of operations is commonly abbreviated as PEMDAS, which stands for Parenthesis, Exponents, Multiplication, Division, Addition, and Subtraction. A mathematical problem containing any of these elements must be solved in the aforementioned sequence.

Let's take a look at each aspect of PEMDAS.

1. Parenthesis

Refers to any content inside of brackets. So, for example, if you had the problem $3 \times 12 \times (4 + 3)$, you would be required to carry out the "4 + 3" within the brackets first. Within the parenthesis, the usual order of operations applies; for example, multiplication within the parenthesis must be carried out before division within the parenthesis, and so forth.

2. Exponents

Refers to the "powers" and "roots" contained within a question. If, for example, you had 3×4^5, you would be required to carry out "4 to the power of 5" before subsequently multiplying by 3.

3. Multiplication

A common slip up to avoid when it comes to the order of operations is incorrectly remembering the order as "PEDMAS" rather than "PEMDAS." If you catch yourself making this error during your practice, be sure to emphasize to yourself that "multiplication is before division" until the correct sequence becomes memorable.

4. Division

The previous point applies here. Always multiply before dividing, and not vice versa.

5. Addition

Addition is one of the aspects of the MST that is often overlooked due to its perceived simplicity. Just because it is a fairly basic aspect of math does not mean it can be overlooked. Being able to carry out rapid, accurate addition is a key component of achieving an excellent result on the MST portion of the test.

6. Subtraction

This should always be your final step, regardless of where the subtraction appears in the sequence of the problem. It can be intuitive to solve a math problem from left to right as written on the page, as this is how English is written. Avoid this. Always refer back to PEMDAS.

Positive & Negative Number Rules

Similar to the order of operations, the rule for dealing with positive and negative numbers is one which may be overlooked when preparing for the MST portion of the ASTB. Let's refresh the basics of this area of math in order to avoid some of the more common errors.

- If you are required to add a positive and a negative number together, subtract the two, and give the sign of the larger initial number to the answer. For example, $20 + -10 = 20 - 10 = 10$.
- If you are required to add two negative numbers, the answer will always be negative. For example, $-10 + -10 = -20$.
- When two negative numbers are multiplied together, the answer is always positive. For example, $-2 \times -2 = 4$
- When one negative and one positive number are multiplied together, the answer is always negative. For example, $4 \times -5 = -20$
- When two negative numbers are divided by each other, the answer is positive. For example, $-20 / -20 = 1$
- When a positive number and a negative number are divided by each other, the answer is always negative. For example, $12 / -2 = -6$

Greatest Common Factor (GCF)

This is the largest whole number that two numbers can be divided by exactly, using a whole number.

Let's use the numbers 40 and 10 as an example; 10 is the largest whole number that both 40 and 10 can be exactly divided by.

Therefore, the Greatest Common Factor of 40 and 10 is 10.

Probability

The ability to calculate the numerical probability of an event is a key part of the MST component to the ASTB.

Probability simply seeks to establish how numerically likely something is to happen.

Let's imagine you have three cars. Two are green, one is not.

If you select a car at random, what is the probability that it is not green? 1 in 3. This is expressed as 1/3.

You are required to simplify probability answers where you can. For example, if you had 100 total cars, and 30 were green, the probability of choosing a green car at random would be 30/100, which can be simplified to 3/10.

Probability can also be expressed as a percentage. Using our above example of 30 green cars out of a total 100 cars, the probability could be expressed as 30% as well as 3/10.

Averages – Mean, Median & Mode

Averages are another aspect of the MST section of the ASTB which are often overlooked due to their perceived simplicity. As ever, making a basic mistake can be the most costly and the most painful type to make. Avoid errors with averages by recapping the following information.

Mean

Mean is a type of average which involves adding together a number of values and then dividing by the number of values given. For example, the mean of 6, 10, and 17 is 11 as (6 + 10 + 17 = 33, and 33/3 = 11).

Median

An average which finds the midpoint between a set of values, after arranging the values in numerical order.

For example, if you are given 3, 5, 24, 89, 102, then the middle value, 24, is the median.

If you have an even number of values, such as 1, 7, 7 and 10, then the two middle values are added together and divided by 2. In this case, the result would be a median of 7 as (7 + 7) /2 = 7.

Mode

The mode is an average which finds the most commonly occurring value in a series of values. For example, from the series 2, 3, 3, 4, 5, 17, the mode is 3. This is due to the fact that the mode occurs more times than any other value.

Algebraic Equations

Algebraic equations can be solved by using different rules of mathematics.

Terms are a product of a number and one or more variables. If a term does not show a coefficient it implies that the coefficient of that term is 1.

Type 1: Addition and Subtraction of like terms

Terms having the same variable can be added and subtracted as per the usual rules of math. For example, $5a + 6a = 11a$ or $12x + 14y - 10x - 18y$ can be combined to form: $2x - 4y$.

Type 2: Multiplication of monomial

The product of 2 or more terms is calculated by multiplying their variables and the coefficients. For example;

$$2x^2y^3z(6x^3yz^4) = 12x^5y^4z^5$$

Type 3: Multiplication of monomial and polynomial

The term outside the bracket is multiplied by all the terms inside the bracket on expansion. The coefficients are multiplied by the coefficients and the variables are multiplied by the variables. For example:

$$2xy^2(3x - 5y + 7x^2y^3) = 6x^2y^2 - 10xy^3 + 14x^3y^5$$

Type 4: Multiplication of binomial with binomial

Each term of the first binomial is multiplied with each term of the other binomial. The coefficients are multiplied by the coefficients and the variables are multiplied by the variables. For example:

$$(2a - 3b)(5ab - 2b^2)$$

$= 10a^2b - 4ab^2 - 15ab^2 + 6b^3$ Like terms can be combined, therefore,

$= 10a^2b - 19ab^2 + 6b^3$

Type 5: Multiplication of binomial with polynomial

Each term of the first binomial is multiplied with each term of the polynomial. The coefficients are multiplied by the coefficients and the variables are multiplied by the variables. For example:

$(a + 2b)(a - 3ab + 4b)$

$= a^2 - 3a^2b + 4ab + 2ab - 6ab^2 + 8b^2$ Like terms can be combined, therefore,

$= a^2 - 3a^2b + 6ab - 6ab^2 + 8b^2$

Distributive Property

A constant, a variable, or a term placed outside the brackets in an equation are multiplied by all the terms in the bracket on expansion. For example:

$7(x - 3y) = 7x - 21y$

$a(4b - 5c) = 4ab - 5ac$

$3a(3b + c) = 9ab + 3ac$

Combining Like Terms

Terms are a product of a variable and a number. Terms with the same variable can be added and subtracted as per the simple rules of mathematics. For example, $4a + 7a = 11a$ or $12x + 14y - 10x - 18y$ can be combined to form: $2x - 4y$.

Arithmetic Series

Arithmetic series is a series in which each successive member of the series differs by a common number. For example, in the arithmetic series of 1, 3, 5, 7, 9…, each successive number differs by 2 from the number that came before it. This common number is sometimes referred to as "common difference." Note: The common difference can also be negative, such as in the case of a series like 25, 22, 19, 16…, here the common difference is -3.

Linear Systems

There are two methods to solve multiple linear equations.

Note: For solving multiple linear equations, the number of known variables must be equal to the number of equations given. For example, 2 unknown variables and 2 equations to solve them:

$x + 3y = 4$ Equation 1

$5x + 6y = 11$ Equation 2

Elimination Method

In the elimination method one equation is manipulated so that the coefficient of one unknown variable becomes equal to the coefficient of the same variable of the other equation.

Here, if Equation 1 is multiplied by 2 it becomes: $2x + 6y = 8$. If this equation is subtracted from Equation 2, the answer is: $3x = 3$. Variable y is eliminated, and the value of x is calculated to be 1. This value of x can be substituted in either Equation 1 or 2, to calculate the value of y which comes out as equal to 1.

Substitution Method

In the substitution method the value of one variable is taken in terms of the other variable using a single equation. This value of the variable is substituted in place of that variable in the other equation. In the given example, Equation 1 can be written as $x = 4 – 3y$. This value of x is substituted in Equation 2:

$5x + 6y = 11$ becomes;

$5(4 – 3y) + 6y = 11$

The solution of this equation yields the value of y to be equal to 1. Since $x = 4 – 3y$, value of x can be calculated to be 1.

The solution of a linear equation is written as, for example, $x = 1, y = 1$

Quadratic Factorization

A quadratic equation can be factorized to calculate the value of the unknown number.

Consider a quadratic equation: $2x^2 - 12x + 18 = 0$. This equation can be solved by using the following steps:

Step 1:

If the coefficient of x and constant number are divisible by the coefficient of x^2, factor it out.

$2(x^2 - 6x + 9) = 0$

$2(x^2 - 6x + 9) = 0$

Step 2:

Find two numbers that are factors of the constant and add up to be equal to the coefficient of x.

Factors of the constant 9 are 3 and -3.

-3 and -3 add up to the coefficient of x = -6

Step 3:

Write down the equation by breaking the coefficient of x in the factors of c.

$2(x^2 - 3x - 3x + 9) = 0$

Step 4:

Take the common numbers in the equation:

$2\{x(x - 3) - 3(x - 3)\} = 0$

$2(x - 3)(x - 3) = 0$

Step 5:

Solve the equation by equating all brackets with zero.

$x - 3 = 0$

$x = 3$

$x - 3 = 0$

$x = 3$

The solution of the equation is x = 3

MST Preparation

The nature of the MST is it is one of the ASTB sections most suited for study and preparation. Math can be practiced in a logical and formulaic way that exposes any gaps in application or understanding, and rectifies them in the most efficient way possible.

One key to preparing for the MST is to not overlook any given concept. Even the more simplistic aspects, such as the order of operations, can prove a pitfall if they are not respected. Do not take any section for granted; instead, be sure to engage with and test your understanding of each and every concept.

Before focusing on the speed at which you solve the problems found on the MST, it is important to first be able to solve the problems in a thorough, logical, and comprehensive manner. The speed at which you solve problems can always be improved upon, but a gap in your process of solving a problem cannot be overcome.

By spending time with the information in this section of the study guide and completing the questions found on the practice test, you should be able to find any glaring weaknesses, such as problems you don't fully understand, let alone have the ability to solve. You will get the most benefit for your effort by first addressing any obvious weak spots before moving on to improving areas of the MST which you have some understanding of.

If any given section proves difficult for you, be sure to do as many problems as possible relating to this topic. For example, if a certain type of algebra is difficult for you, do as many questions relating to it as you can. Search the internet for even more practice questions. However, don't just carry out practice aiming to get the right answer. Instead, it is vital you understand **why** an answer is right or wrong. You should always write out your full work and understanding as this will expose any gaps in your logic and process.

You should also consider watching YouTube videos showing examples of math problems. Sometimes watching the way someone else solves a problem will show you a better way of doing it, or make you realize there is a step you misunderstood, or you are carrying out in the wrong order.

MST Practice Test

1. I spend a third of my money on a book, half of the rest on a gun and a quarter of what I then have left on a t-shirt. What proportion of my original money do I have left?

    A. 66%
    B. 50%
    C. 33%
    D. 25%

2. $12x - 5y = -20$, $y = x+4$

    A. $x = 2$ $y = 4$
    B. $x = -2$ $y = 5$
    C. $x = 0$ $y = 4$
    D. $x = 20$ $y = -2$

3. You get a pay bump of 4% plus an extra $5 per week. You currently make $250 per week. How much is your new level of income after the pay bump?

    A. $265
    B. $260
    C. $255
    D. $254

4. Find the nth term of the sequence -1, 2, 9, 20

    A. $n^2 - 3n$
    B. $2n^2 - 3n$
    C. $2n^2 - 2n - 1$
    D. $2n^2 - n - 2$

5. $2y + 3x = 38$ $y - 2x = 12$

    A. $x = 2$, $y = 16$
    B. $x = 4$, $y = 22$
    C. $x = 5$, $y = 6$
    D. $x = 12$, $y = 3$

6. If you divide two negative numbers together, the answer is always

    A. Positive
    B. Negative
    C. Can be either positive or negative
    D. 0

7. $x^2 + 9x + 18$

    A. $(x + 5) (x + 4)$
    B. $(x + 2) (x + 9)$
    C. $(x + 6) (x + 3)$
    D. $(x + 2) (x + 10)$

8. There is a wooden post in a frozen area. Half of the post is embedded in the ground, another one third is covered by snow, and 7 feet is out in the air. What is the total length of the pole?

    A. 32 feet
    B. 42 feet
    C. 40 feet
    D. 21 feet

9. $15r - 10 - (-7r) + 5r + 3$

    A. 20 r + 13
    B. 27 r - 7
    C. 3 r - 13
    D. 22 r + 7

10. Find the next two numbers in the sequence 2, 8, 18, 32, _, _

    A. 46, 60
    B. 42, 52
    C. 50, 72
    D. 100, 121

11. If a clock's hour hand moves $1/60^{th}$ of a degree every minute, how many degrees will it move in an hour?

    A. 60
    B. 1
    C. 30
    D. 20

12. Total height of a class is 1300 cm. If the average height of a class is 65 cm, find the number of students in the class.

    A. 24
    B. 20
    C. 18
    D. 16

13. To the nearest cubic inch, how much dirt is there in a 3ft × 2ft × 2ft hole?

    A. 12 cubic inches
    B. 144 cubic inches
    C. 120 cubic inches
    D. 0 cubic inches

14. $3 + 2 + 7t - 4t$

    A. 11t - 5
    B. 3t + 5
    C. t + 5
    D. 12 t + 5

15. When asked her age, Jess replied, "In two years I will be twice as old as I was five years ago." How old is she?

    A. 6
    B. 20
    C. 12
    D. 8

16. The average consumption of wheat by a family member is 33 lbs in three months. If there are 15 members in the family, find the total consumption for three months.

    A. 495 lbs
    B. 480 lbs
    C. 505 lbs
    D. 320 lbs

17. The final stage in the order of operations is

    A. Addition
    B. Multiplication
    C. Division
    D. Subtraction

18. Find the average of 3.6, 2.7, 4.1, 1.5, and 5.3

    A. 3.42
    B. 3.44
    C. 3.4
    D. 3.46

19. Adding two negative numbers

    A. Always results in a negative number
    B. Always results in a positive number
    C. Can result in either a negative or positive number
    D. Results in 0

20. Solve $x^2 - 7x = 0$.

    A. x = 0, 7
    B. x = 13, 1
    C. x = 7, 1
    D. x= 0, 1

MST Answer Key

1. D
2. C
3. A
4. B
5. A
6. A
7. C
8. B
9. B
10. C
11. B
12. B
13. D
14. B
15. C
16. A
17. D
18. B
19. A
20. A

Reading Comprehension Test (RCT)

RCT Purpose

At first glance, the RCT may seem like less of an obvious choice for the ASTB than some of the other sections. For example, it is easy to understand the reason why a future aviator must have a solid grasp of the physics of flight or the safety markings found in an airport, as found in the ANIT portion of the ASTB. Being able to interpret passages of text, however, is a skill less obviously suited to a military career.

So why exactly are ASTB students required to undertake this portion of the ASTB? There are two main reasons why the RCT portion of the ASTB is used by the Navy: first, a lot of instructions over the course of a military career will come in written form, so it's essential to be proficient at interpreting language to make sure you understand what it's really saying. Misunderstanding a written instruction during an actual Naval career could lead to a severely grave error. The other reason why the RCT is valued by the Navy is it indicates a person's general intelligence.

Although it is unlikely that you will ever be required to do the type of problems required by the RCT during your actual career in the Navy, its importance cannot be overlooked. This is especially true if you are a technically or mathematically minded person. The type of word logic required for the RCT is something you may not have had reason to practice for a long time. If this is the case, it's vitally important to practice the technique found in this section of the study guide and to apply it to the practice text, noting any aspect of the test you find particularly difficult, and working methodically to improve upon it.

RCT Contents

Subject vs Main Idea

When preparing for the RCT portion of the ASTB, it is vital to think of the text extracts as containing both a topic and a main idea. The topic is simply the subject or content of the paragraph, whereas the main idea is the opinion, judgement, or assertion that the writer is making about the topic. Sometimes, paragraphs will be informative rather than opinionated, and the writer will not offer a strong opinion. In paragraphs where an opinion is given, however, it is vital to be able to distinguish this from the purely informative content.

Let's take a look at an example of this distinction.

"Of all the food that people can eat, junk food is a popular choice for many. In spite of its prevalence, junk food can cause a number of health problems for those who eat it. This can be seen as negative for the following reasons…"

In the above example, the topic is food, and junk food in particular. However, the writer goes on to say that junk food is negative. This is an opinion, and the main idea the writer wants to convey.

This distinction will help you avoid one of the key pitfalls that comes with the RCT portion of the ASTB. Many people, when considering their answer choices during the process of elimination, mistakenly gravitate towards any sentence that has to do with the topic. They recognize the presence of language referring to the topic of the paragraph, without stopping to consider whether it relates to the main idea as stated by the question.

Topic Sentences

It is common, but not universal, to find a single sentence that expresses the main idea of a paragraph in a nutshell. This is referred to as a "topic sentence." Not all paragraphs contain a topic sentence, but for those that do, it is one of the most useful hints in answering an RCT question. Topic sentences are often, but not always, found at the start of a text extract. Consider the following:

"Naval information gathering missions are dangerous, as clearly shown by the fact that …"

This single sentence reveals a wealth of information about the text extract to follow. We know that the topic of the paragraph will be naval information gathering missions.

We also know that the main idea being put forward by the writer is that such missions are dangerous, and that the writer will go on to show a number of reasons why this is the case.

As stated, topic sentences do not have to be placed at the beginning of the paragraph. They can also be used as a way of finishing a paragraph. Take a look at the following:

"A career in the military combines the opportunity for growth, service, and pushing your personal boundaries in a way that almost no other career can. For this reason, it is the greatest career choice a person can make."

As shown in the above extract, it is possible for a writer to state their reasons for holding a certain opinion before concluding with their topic sentence, their main idea. How can this be applied? Basically, if you are considering a text passage in the RCT, and you are checking to see whether it has a topic sentence, be sure to look at both the start and the end of the text. A topic sentence may be found in either position.

It's possible to come across a text section of the RCT that lacks a single topic sentence but does contain a main idea nonetheless. Consider the following passage:

"America is full of places containing beautiful scenery. The people are friendly, helpful, and neighborly. The cuisine and culture offered has something to suit every taste imaginable."

Would you agree that the above passage contains the main idea that America is positive? Although this isn't expressed in the form of a single sentence, it nonetheless is conveyed by the three separate ideas about America, each of which focuses on a different praiseworthy aspect of the nation. If you are trying to find a main idea without the benefit of a single topic sentence, look for a common assertion or theme, which can be deduced when each of the sentences of the text extract are considered in turn.

Making Use Of Context And Understanding Unknown Language

Sometimes, you will come across a question in the RCT portion of the ASTB that contains a strange or uncommon word. This is done in order to test your ability to find the meaning of a word based on the context in which it is found. In other words, you are required to look at the sentences and words around the new, unknown word, in order to determine what it is likely to mean.

Consider the following:

"The truck yard was filled with a loud and infuriating mixture of noises. They mixed together about as well as oil and water. The harsh clashing of metal being pounded against metal, the rusty desperation of old engines trying to spring to life, the dry and dusty coughs of dry and dusty men. He was perturbed by the cacophony that he encountered."

Let's imagine that you had not encountered the word cacophony before. Cacophony refers to an unpleasant mixture of sounds and noises that do not belong together – an unorganized, nasty mixture of noises. Imagine having to define cacophony using one of the following three options:

a.   A truck
b.   A noise
c.   A harsh and horrible mix of sounds

By looking at the three options given, and then looking back at the text, it is advisable to begin a process of contextual information. By reading each answer in turn, and then weighing it up against the context of the text, it is possible to start eliminating ideas that don't fit.

Looking first at option a), we know that trucks are in fact mentioned in the text, as the location for it is a truck yard. However, at no point is an actual truck mentioned. Therefore, it seems unlikely that truck will be the meaning of cacophony here. Next, consider option b). Although the text passage does indeed mention noise, and different noises, option b) specifically specifies a single noise. We know that the text mentions many noises. Therefore, it is unlikely that option b) will be a good fit. If we look at option c), a harsh and horrible mix of sounds, we will find much in the text passage to suggest this is in fact the correct option. The text mentions many different sounds, and the language it uses to describe them is not pleasant or positive. When weighing all three options against the contents of the text, we will certainly reach the conclusion that option c) is the best fit in this case.

The Language Of Cause And Effect

There are certain types of language that are signposts toward the idea a writer is trying to convey. This is especially helpful in the case where a text extract does not contain a single topic sentence, and the main idea must therefore be deduced. Consider the following as an example, with the signpost language highlighted in bold:

"With a young, fairly inexperienced group of players, a coach without much of a track record of winning, and a slew of injuries to the squad, things could hardly be tougher for the team. **Therefore,** no one had high expectations for them heading into the season. However, much to…"

This paragraph is an example of when a text's main idea is found in the middle without a clear topic sentence to indicate it. The writer gives some supporting information, which combines and adds up together, building until the word therefore. After therefore, the writer makes a concluding point, which is the sum of the information that came before it. Therefore is a way of saying "because of what has just been stated, this is what I think." If you see therefore in an RCT passage, you have found a great shortcut to understanding the writer's main idea for that section.

Consequently is another useful cause and effect word that acts as a way to determine the main idea in an RCT extract. It basically means "as a consequence of" and is used to state a main idea following a series of supporting statements. Consider the following passage:

"Luke had been eating far too much as of late. His loneliness and depression had led to him finding solace and comfort in delicious, fattening food. **Consequently,** his health and looks were at an all-time low point. His appearance was unappealing…"

Here we can see that the writer uses consequently to give the idea that "due to the things I have just said, this is the assertion I am making." Another way of stating this would be "as a result of the food consumption and emotional factors behind it, Luke has the outcome of bad health and an ugly appearance." Consequently shows us this.

Sometimes, more than one answer choice may seem to be correct for an RCT question, and the thing determining which is actually right comes down to the usage of a single word. This word choice is often as subtle and hard to detect as it is influential.

Consider the massive difference in meaning in the following two examples, despite the fact that the language used is almost identical, except for one small choice of word:

"The building was affordable and perfectly suited to its purpose. Its location was everything they had ever hoped for. In spite of its young age, they wouldn't change it for the world."

"The building was well inside their budget and fulfilled all of their requirements. They were very happy with its location, which was exactly as they had wished. Despite it being advanced in years, they couldn't be happier with the building."

In both of the above extracts, the writer is talking about a building. The language is more or less the same, conveying the same positive qualities about the building's location and other aspects. If you read them both carefully, you will notice that the only real difference between them is the age of the building. In the first extract the building is described as having a "young age," whereas in the second the building is described as "advanced in years." Only a few words differ, but a key piece of information about the building is drastically different from passage to passage.

This idea, and the examples illustrating it, teach us a key lesson about the RCT portion of the ASTB. Firstly, questions may hinge on a few words, a single word, or even part of a word. Sometimes, the way to determine the difference between possible answer choices will come down to even a prefix or a suffix, such as the presence of -im or -un before a word, making it negative in meaning. As a result of this, it is important to remain calm under pressure and read the passage as slowly and carefully as possible. Failing to pick up on something as small as a few different words, or a word with a meaning altering prefix, can result in you choosing a wrong answer when the correct choice would have been apparent after more careful consideration.

RCT Technique – Process Of Elimination

Our suggested way to approach an RCT question is to read the series of answer choices you are provided first before even looking at the actual text extract. This is due to the fact that the options you are presented with will inform your reading of the text, as certain answer choices will require you to look for the presence, or absence, of certain language. Consider the following four answers:

a. Setting deadlines is always easy.
b. Setting deadlines is never easy.
c. Setting deadlines is easier for some people than others.
d. Bosses are always understanding when a deadline needs to be extended.

By first reading these four answer options, you would have a clear idea of the type of language you need to look for when reading the passage of text itself. For example, in this case, you would look at language related to the ease of deadlines, language related to whether the setting of deadlines differs from person to person, and any language referencing bosses and the way in which they deal with deadlines.

After you have first read your answer choices, and then the text they correspond to, it is important to try and eliminate the least likely answers first. Let's use the same a), b), c), and d) answer choices as above and imagine they correspond to the following passage:

"Deadlines are a fact of life for almost every project, but that doesn't mean they are always easy, straightforward, or pain free. Some people do not find it difficult to set and stick to deadlines, while others find it one of the hardest aspects of their work. That's before you even start to factor in the range of responses that bosses may have to a missed or extended deadline."

We'll now go through this passage in the sequence in which it is written in order to illustrate a process of elimination, which you are advised to use for the RCT portion of the ASTB. In the first sentence, we come across the assertion "that doesn't mean they are always easy." On the basis of this assertion, we are able to eliminate option a), setting deadlines is always easy. Reading on, we come across the assertion that "some people do not find it difficult to set and stick to deadlines." As this refers to only "some" people, we can deduce that some people do in fact find it hard to set and stick to deadlines. This eliminates option b), as we know that sometimes deadlines are in fact easy.

Continuing reading, we find the assertion that there are a "range of responses that bosses may have to a missed or extended deadline." This eliminates option d), as it is clear that bosses will not always respond in a certain way to a missed or extended deadline, which would have to be the case for option d) to be correct. This process of elimination reveals the correct option to be option c), which aside from the process of elimination, is further supported by the language found in the passage.

There are two strategies that are advised to be used in the RCT section of the ASTB. Both require reading the answer choices first. You should experiment with both options in order to find the one that works best for you.

The first option is the one shown above, which involves going through the text a sentence at a time, and seeing which options can be eliminated on the basis of the assertions that the writer has made. Let's look at another example of this method of approaching an RCT question. Consider the following answer choices:

a. Daniel is tall
b. Daniel is unemployed
c. Daniel is miserable
d. Daniel has a pet

"Daniel woke up, dwarfed by the single bed in which his 5 foot 4 frame rested. He was in a rush, as he had to be at the office within the hour, or risk unemployment due to his recent final warning from the company. Despite this pressure, a smile was on his face, and he felt good about the day ahead. The sound of his beloved dog greeting him, demanding breakfast, further made the start of his day delightful."

By reading through the text in order, we are able to eliminate some of the answer choices as we go. This requires the use of synonyms and logic in order to interpret and comprehend the information given. In the first sentence, there are two things which allow us to eliminate answer choice a). First of all, we come across the word dwarfed, which shows that Daniel appears small in comparison to a single bed. As we know that a single bed is not a large bed, we can deduce that Daniel is not a tall person.

Second, we are explicitly given his height, which most people would be able to determine is not the height of a tall person. Reading on, we discover that Daniel will "risk" unemployment if he is not on time. From this information, we can tell that Daniel is currently employed, which eliminates answer b). Further reading shows that Daniel is smiling and feeling good, which shows that he is not miserable, eliminating answer choice c). Finally, we see reference to a dog, which proves answer choice d) is in fact the correct option.

The other option you may wish to try out aside from the above process is to read each answer choice one at a time, scan the text, and then read the next option, scan the text, and so on. This has the advantage of allowing you to look for language only related to one answer at a time, which can be useful if you are struggling to consider the text as a whole in light of all of the answer choices given. However, this method often takes more time, as it requires four readings of the text. Try both ways and see if one is more suited to you than the other in terms of finding the correct answer, and doing so within the time allotted for each question on the RCT portion of the ASTB.

RCT Preparation

Your preparation for the RCT should have two ultimate aims: to improve your speed and to improve your understanding by identifying and eliminating any particular weaknesses or struggles you have.

It'd advised that your first focus is to work on accuracy rather than speed. This is due to the fact that it is possible to improve your speed further down the line. It's better to get a solid understanding of the technique first, before hastening it later.

Aside from working through the methods and examples given in this section of your ASTB study guide, and answering the practice test section under timed conditions, there are other ways in which you can give yourself an advantage on the RCT portion of the ASTB.

It's essential to read as much as you can. By reading, either fiction or nonfiction, you will encounter a greater variety of language and words and therefore become more familiar with possible synonyms and unusual language that you may encounter on the ASTB.

It's important to not just read, but read intelligently. When reading in light of the RCT, you should be constantly engaging with the words you encounter, considering their synonyms and antonyms. Be sure to always check the meaning of any unfamiliar words, and consider the way in which they are used.

It's also a good idea to diversify the material you read. If you read the same type of writing again and again, or the same publications, you risk limiting yourself and being unprepared for the type of language you may encounter on the ASTB. Try and read news from different sources, different types of fiction, and different types of nonfiction.

RCT Practice Test

1. Now having a night, a day, and still another night following before me in New Bedford before I could embark for my destined port, it became a matter of concernment where I was to eat and sleep meanwhile. It was a very dubious-looking, nay, dark, and dismal night, bitingly cold and cheerless.

    A. The eventual aim of the journey is unknown
    B. The weather is pleasant
    C. The man has one more night in his current location
    D. The man will leave after two nights have passed

2. The next thing wanted was to get the picture framed, and here were a few difficulties. It must be done directly; it must be done in London; the order must go through the hands of some intelligent person whose taste could be depended on; and Isabella, the usual doer of all commissions, must not be applied to, because it was December, and Mr. Woodhouse could not bear the idea of her stirring out of her house in the fogs of December. But no sooner was the distress known to Mr. Elton, than it was removed.

    A. The picture can be framed in many cities
    B. Isabella is the best choice for the job
    C. There is one month until the new year
    D. Mr. Elton did not help the situation

3. It was close upon four before the door opened, and a drunken-looking groom, ill-kempt and side-whiskered, with an inflamed face and disreputable clothes, walked into the room. Accustomed as I was to my friend's amazing powers in the use of disguises, I had to look three times before I was certain that it was indeed he. With a nod, he vanished into the bedroom, whence he emerged in five minutes tweed-suited and respectable, as of old. Putting his hands into his pockets, he stretched out his legs in front of the fire and laughed heartily for some minutes.

    A. The friend is in a somber mood
    B. The friend has worn disguises before
    C. A tweed suit is not a respectable look
    D. The friend did not gesture before moving into the bedroom

4. Ignorance is the parent of fear, and being completely nonplussed and confounded about the stranger, I confess I was now as much afraid of him as if it was the devil himself who had thus broken into my room at the dead of night. In fact, I was so

afraid of him that I was not game enough just then to address him, and demand a satisfactory answer concerning what seemed inexplicable in him.

- A. A lack of knowledge precedes fear
- B. The writer is afraid of an acquaintance
- C. The writer feels capable of speaking to the other man
- D. There is a strong mutual fear

5. He was lounging upon the sofa in a purple dressing-gown, a pipe-rack within his reach upon the right, and a pile of crumpled morning papers, evidently newly studied, near at hand. Beside the couch was a wooden chair, and on the angle of the back hung a very seedy and disreputable hard-felt hat, much the worse for wear and cracked in several places. A lens and a pair of forceps lying upon the seat of the chair suggested that the hat had been suspended in this manner for the purpose of examination.

- A. The hat is new
- B. The man is dressed formally
- C. The man is illiterate
- D. The man is relaxed

6. This letter, however, was written, and sealed, and sent. The business was finished, and Harriet safe. She was rather low all the evening, but Emma could allow for her amiable regrets, and sometimes relieved them by speaking of her own affection, sometimes by bringing forward the idea of Mr. Elton.

- A. Harriet is in danger
- B. Emma never feels relief
- C. The written correspondence has been sent
- D. The letter has been responded to

7. Above the woods which lined it upon the farther side, we could see the red, jutting pinnacles which marked the site of the rich landowner's dwelling. On the Hatherley side of the pool the woods grew very thick, and there was a narrow belt of sodden grass twenty paces across between the edge of the trees and the reeds which lined the lake. Lestrade showed us the exact spot at which the body had been found, and, indeed, so moist was the ground, that I could plainly see the traces which had been left by the fall of the stricken man.

- A. The trees are sparse
- B. A murder has occurred
- C. The grass is wet
- D. The owner of the land is in poverty

8. Mr. Knightley might quarrel with her, but Emma could not quarrel with herself. He was so much displeased, that it was longer than usual before he came to Hartfield again; and when they did meet, his grave looks shewed that she was not forgiven. She was sorry, but could not repent. On the contrary, her plans and proceedings were more and more justified and endeared to her by the general appearances of the next few days.

    A. The man's feelings are apparent by his expression
    B. Emma regrets her intended plans
    C. Emma is acting without justification
    D. Emma is planning a long journey

9. Josiah, my father, married young, and carried his wife with three children into New England, about 1682. The conventicles, having been forbidden by law and frequently disturbed, induced some considerable men of his acquaintance to remove to that country, and he was prevailed with to accompany them thither, where they expected to enjoy their mode of religion with freedom. By the same wife, he had four children more born there, and by a second wife ten more, in all seventeen; of which I remember thirteen sitting at one time at his table, who all grew up to be men and women, and married.

    A. Some of the thirteen children died before adulthood
    B. Freedom to practice religion was worldwide at the time
    C. The man had only one wife
    D. People migrated for reasons of freedom

10. In the evening, I found myself very feverish, and went in to bed; but, having read somewhere that cold water drank plentifully was good for a fever, I followed the prescription, sweat plentifully most of the night, my fever left me, and in the morning, crossing the ferry, I proceeded on my journey on foot, having fifty miles to Burlington, where I was told I should find boats that would carry me the rest of the way to Philadelphia.

    A. The man has been told in conversation to drink water
    B. The man is aiming to end up in Philadelphia
    C. The man did not have enough cold water
    D. Cold water worsens a fever

11. The lawyers gathered together down in front of the steps and discussed with each other what they should do; on the one hand, they had actually no right to be allowed into the building so that there was hardly anything that they could legally

do to the official and, as I've already mentioned, they would have to be careful not to set all the officials against them. On the other hand, any day not spent in court is a day lost for them and it was a matter of some importance to force their way inside. In the end, they agreed that they would try to tire the old man out. One lawyer after another was sent out to run up the steps and let himself be thrown down again, offering what resistance he could as long as it was passive resistance, and his colleagues would catch him at the bottom of the steps. That went on for about an hour until the old gentleman, who was already exhausted from working all night, was very tired and went back to his office.

 A. The lawyers were legally allowed in the courtroom
 B. The lawyers actively resisted being thrown
 C. The old man was initially feeling energetic
 D. The lawyers' plan succeeded

12. From a child, I was fond of reading, and all the little money that came into my hands was ever laid out in books. Pleased with the *Pilgrim's Progress*, my first collection was of John Bunyan's works in separate little volumes. I afterward sold them to enable me to buy R. Burton's *Historical Collections*; they were small books, and cheap, 40 or 50 in all. My father's little library consisted chiefly of books in polemic divinity, most of which I read, and have since often regretted that, at a time when I had such a thirst for knowledge, more proper books had not fallen in my way, since it was now resolved I should not be a clergyman.

 A. There is a chance the writer will join the clergy
 B. The writer did not like the cost of books
 C. The writer's father had books about religion
 D. The writer lost his love of reading over time

13. He gave me the impression that he was repeating something which he had learned by heart or that, magnetized by some words of his own speech, his mind was slowly circling round and round in the same orbit. At times, he spoke as if he were simply alluding to some fact that everybody knew, and at times he lowered his voice and spoke mysteriously as if he were telling us something secret which he did not wish others to overhear. He repeated his phrases over and over again, varying them and surrounding them with his monotonous voice. I continued to gaze towards the foot of the slope, listening to him.

 A. The speaker speaks in a consistent tone
 B. The writer does not listen to the speaker
 C. The speaker has a lively voice
 D. The speaker's voice lacks variety

14. The temptation for once to turn the job down was very great, especially as it had no direct connection with business, but there was no denying that social obligations towards this business contact were in themselves important enough, only not for K., who knew quite well that he needed some successes at work if he was to maintain his position there and that, if he failed in that, it would not help him even if this Italian somehow found him quite charming; he did not want to be removed from his workplace for even one day, as the fear of not being allowed back in was too great; he knew full well that the fear was exaggerated but it still made him anxious.

   A. The man is concerned about his employment security
   B. The man's fears are rational and fully justified
   C. The man is meeting someone from Africa
   D. The man does not think social obligations matter

15. She looked around the room, reviewing all its familiar objects which she had dusted once a week for so many years, wondering where on earth all the dust came from. Perhaps she would never see again those familiar objects from which she had never dreamed of being divided. And yet during all those years she had never found out the name of the priest whose yellowing photograph hung on the wall above the broken harmonium beside the colored print of the promises made to Blessed Margaret Mary Alacoque. He had been a school friend of her father. Whenever he showed the photograph to a visitor, her father used to pass it with a casual word.

   A. The Priest is on first name terms with the woman
   B. The Priest had known her father at college
   C. The woman carried out regular care of her possessions
   D. The woman always expected to be parted from her possessions

16. The air in the room was fuggy and extremely oppressive, those who were standing furthest away could hardly even be seen through it. It must have been especially troublesome for those visitors who were in the gallery, as they were forced to quietly ask the participants in the assembly what exactly was happening, albeit with timid glances at the judge. The replies they received were just as quiet, and given behind the protection of a raised hand.

   A. The judge is looked at boldly and rudely
   B. The room feels pleasant
   C. The room is empty
   D. The text is set in a court

17. Two young men came down the hill of Rutland Square. One of them was just bringing a long monologue to a close. The other, who walked on the verge of the path and was at times obliged to step on to the road, owing to his companion's rudeness, wore an amused listening face. He was squat and ruddy. A yachting cap was shoved far back from his forehead and the narrative to which he listened made constant waves of expression break forth over his face from the corners of his nose and eyes and mouth. Little jets of wheezing laughter followed one another out of his convulsed body. His eyes, twinkling with cunning enjoyment, glanced at every moment towards his companion's face.

    A. The men converse with one another
    B. The man reacts to the story with his facial expression
    C. Both men are tall and strong
    D. The men are jogging

18. He did not feel at all like going to bed, so he decided to stay up, and this would also give him the chance to find out when Miss Bürstner would arrive home. Perhaps it would also still be possible, even if a little inappropriate, to have a few words with her. As he lay there by the window, pressing his hands to his tired eyes, he even thought for a moment that he might punish Mrs. Grubach by persuading Miss Bürstner to give in her notice at the same time as he would. But he immediately realized that that would be shockingly excessive, and there would even be the suspicion that he was moving house because of the incidents of that morning.

    A. The man's mind was blank
    B. The man decided his plans were too severe
    C. The man tried to sleep but could not
    D. The room was windowless

19. He threw himself down on his bed, and from the dressing table he took the nice apple that he had put there the previous evening for his breakfast. Now it was all the breakfast he had and anyway, as he confirmed as soon as he took his first, big bite of it, it was far better than a breakfast he could have had through the good will of the policemen from the dirty café. He felt well and confident; he had failed to go into work at the bank this morning but that could easily be excused because of the relatively high position he held there.

    A. The man holds an entry level job
    B. The man cautiously nibbles his breakfast
    C. The man feels positive
    D. The man is allergic to fruit

20. Though his eyes took note of many elements of the crowd through which he passed, they did so morosely. He found trivial all that was meant to charm him and did not answer the glances which invited him to be bold. He knew that he would have to speak a great deal, to invent and to amuse, and his brain and throat were too dry for such a task. The problem of how he could pass the hours until he met Corley again troubled him a little. He could think of no way of passing them but to keep on walking. He turned to the left when he came to the corner of Rutland Square and felt more at ease in the dark quiet street, the somber look of which suited his mood.

    A. The man is physically ready to impress verbally
    B. The man is blind in one eye
    C. The man's surroundings match the way he feels
    D. The man is planning a crime

RCT Answer Key

1. D
2. C
3. B
4. A
5. D
6. C
7. C
8. A
9. D
10. B
11. D
12. C
13. D
14. A
15. C
16. D
17. B
18. B
19. C
20. C

Aviation and Nautical Information Test (ANIT)

ANIT Purpose

The Aviation and Nautical Information section of the ASTB has the most direct relevance to your future Navy career. Unlike more abstract test sections such as the RCT and MST, the ANIT tests your understanding of concepts you will use in your day to day Navy life, such as the different types of military craft and what they do, how to navigate an airport safely, and the proud history of the Navy itself.

The ANIT is the section of the ASTB which requires the most knowledge. Not only that, but depending on your background, a lot of the information is likely to be new. It is therefore often the section of the ASTB which requires the greatest focus of your time and energy while preparing for the test.

Due to the vast amount of knowledge required for success on the ANIT, it is absolutely essential to make a careful plan to ensure that you cover all of the material in time. Divide the contents up into topics and further into sub topics. It is better to understand all of the topics at an 80% level than it is to understand a few of them perfectly, and some of them not at all.

Serving in the Navy is an honor, and this section, above all others, prepares you for the prestige of the role. By respecting the history and traditions of the institution in which you will serve, you begin to have the right mentality to represent the Navy in the most honorable way possible.

ANIT Contents

Airports

Taxiways

Familiarity with the layout of an airport and the markings used is highly advantageous both for the ASTB and for a future military career.

A taxiway is the route which an aircraft is permitted to travel when travelling to or from a runway. A taxiway uses yellow markings. The edges of the taxiway are indicated by two parallel, solid yellow lines, and the centerline is a single solid yellow line.

A taxiway also has holding lines which run across the width of the taxiway. Holding lines are two sets of solid yellow lines and two sets of dashed yellow lines, which indicate when an aircraft must wait for permission to proceed along the taxiway.

Hold position signs located along taxiways are red with white characters, and indicate aspects of airport functioning such as no entry for restricted areas, runway hold positions, and runway approach hold positions.

Runway Markings

The displaced threshold is the start of the landing portion of a runway. It is marked by white arrows pointing toward vertical white lines.

Yellow chevrons designate an area of a runway which is unsuitable for landings, takeoff, and taxiing, unless in the case of an emergency.

A large white X symbol indicates that a runway is unusable.

Airport Lighting

Lighting is intended to ensure that pilots are able to operate aircraft safely within the airport during the night or times of low visibility.

Taxiways are lit by green lighting placed along the centerline, blue lighting marking the edges, or a combination of the two at the discretion of the airport operator.

Runways are lit by white lines along the sides, designating the edges of the runway. The ends of runways are lit by red and green lights. Red lights face the runway end, whereas green lights face the runway threshold.

Runway obstructions are indicated by omnidirectional (facing every direction) red lighting.

Visual approach slope indicators, commonly abbreviated as VASI, are systems of lights that inform a pilot of the correct approach during a descent. If a pilot is descending correctly, then they will see an even number of red and white lights. If all the lights are white, the pilot is flying too high. If all the lights are red, the pilot is flying too low.

Aircraft Right Of Way

The right of way of aircraft is one of the most important aspects of safe aviation.

If an aircraft is in distress, then it automatically has the right of way, no matter what other circumstances are at play.

If two aircraft approach each other head on, both should give way to the right.

If one aircraft is overtaking another, the faster aircraft must pass the slower aircraft on the right side and leave a sufficiently safe gap while doing so.

If two aircraft's routes converge, the craft on the right side has the right of way, provided they are the same category of aircraft.

If aircraft of different categories converge, then the least maneuverable aircraft has the right of way. The hierarchy of maneuverability, from least to most maneuverable, is as follows:

Balloon, Glider, Refueling Aircraft, Airship, Airplane or Rotorcraft

If aircraft are approaching for landing at the same time, then the craft flying at the lower altitude has right of way over the aircraft flying at the higher altitude.

Airspace Classifications

Airspace within the USA is classified according to the following conventions: MSL refers to Mean Sea Level, FL refers to Flight Level, and AGL refers to Above Ground Level.

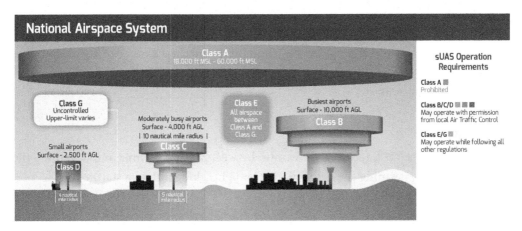

Class A – 18,000 ft MSL up to FL600

Class B – surface to 10,000 ft MSL, surrounds major airports

Class C – surface to 4,000 ft AGL, around busy airports

Class D – surface to 2,500 ft AGL, surrounds airports with operational control tower

Class G – surface to either 1,200 ft AGL or 700 ft AGL

Class E – everything else

Aircraft Axis

An aircraft moves along three axes: longitudinal, lateral, and vertical.

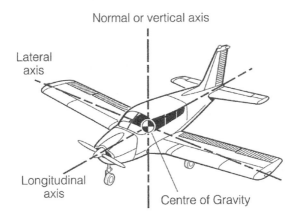

The longitudinal axis of a plane runs along the fuselage, typically depicted as the nose to the tail of the plane. This axis provides the aircraft with lateral stability. Banking, or rolling, is the aircraft movement which occurs along this axis.

The lateral axis runs from one wing of the plane to the other and provides longitudinal stability. Pitching is the aircraft movement which occurs along this axis.

The vertical axis runs from the top to the bottom of the fuselage of the plane. The vertical axis is sometimes called the "yaw axis," as yawing is the aircraft movement occurring along this axis.

Measurements

A nautical mile is 6,076 feet long. The ratio between a nautical mile and a statute mile (and mile) is 8/7, meaning the nautical mile is slightly longer than a statute mile.

Gasoline weighs 6 lbs per gallon.

Oil weighs 7.5 lbs per gallon.

Water weighs 8.35 lbs per gallon.

Key Ship Terminology

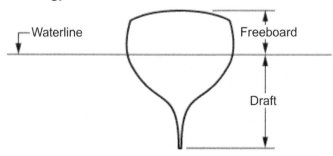

Freeboard is the area between the water level of a ship and the lowest portion of the deck where water could enter.

Draft is the area between the water level and the base of the ship.

The deck of a ship is divided into halves. The forecastle is the bow half of the deck, while the fantail is the stern half of the deck.

The keel is the major structural component of a ship, running along the middle of the vessel from bow to stern. This is the initial component of a ship to which all else is later attached.

Navigation

Dead reckoning refers to the method of navigation which consists of using a compass and nothing else. Due to this limitation, it is sometimes thought of as an educated guess.

Terrain association is a method of navigation by which surrounding terrain features are used to determine the correct course to take.

Ship Naming Conventions

CV & CVN	Aircraft carriers, "n" indicating nuclear powered
LPH, LHA, LHD	Amphibious assault ships
LCC	Amphibious command ships
LPD	Amphibious transport docks
SSBN, SSGN	Ballistic missile submarines
CG	Cruisers
DDG	Destroyers
LSD	Dock landing ships
T-Ake	Dry cargo ships
SSN	Fast attack submarines
AOE	Fast combat support ships
FFG	Frigates
LCS	Littoral combat ships
MCM	Mine countermeasures ships
PC	Patrol boats
T-AO	Replenishment oilers

Weather & Atmosphere

Atmosphere Layers

Troposphere   0–7 miles above the surface of the Earth

Stratosphere   7–31 miles above the surface of the Earth

Mesosphere   31–50 miles above the surface of the Earth

Thermosphere   50–440 miles above the surface of the Earth

Exosphere   440–3,200 miles above the surface of the Earth

Chemical Aspects of Air

Air consists of roughly 78% nitrogen, 21% oxygen, and 1% argon. It also contains traces of carbon dioxide and hydrogen.

When a pilot operates at 10,000 ft above the Earth or higher, they typically require an oxygen supply.

Drag Types

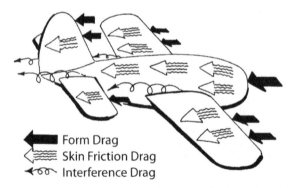

→ Form Drag
→ Skin Friction Drag
→ Interference Drag

Parasite – Parasite drag is a combination of form drag, interference drag, and skin friction drag. It occurs because the solid object (airplane) is passing through a fluid medium, which in this case, is the atmosphere.

Form – Drag resulting from the shape of the plane. Planes with a thicker cross section have higher levels of form drag, whereas planes with a thinner cross section have lower levels of form drag.

Interference – Occurs when varied currents of air over an airplane meet and interact.

Skin Friction – Very small amounts of roughness on the material used to make the plane cause air to pass over it less smoothly, resulting in skin friction.

Induced – Induced drag results from the lift generated by the wing.

Total Drag – Sum of parasite and induced drag.

Naval History

1775, 10/13 – Official establishment of the Continental Navy

1794 – Naval Act led to the creation of the United States Navy

1805 – Successful Battle of Derna, Tripoli sees the American flag raised on foreign soil for the first time

1900 – The first submarine is commissioned into the US Navy, the USS Holland IV (SS-1)

1910, 11/14 – Naval Aviation begins when Eugene Ely takes off from the USS Birmingham and lands safely on shore

1939 – US Navy ships begin patrolling the Atlantic Ocean for German submarines

1942 – Damage inflicted on Japanese carriers during the Battle of Midway is considered the turning point in the Pacific War

1975 – USS Mayaguez is rescued swiftly from Cambodia by Navy and Marine Corps

1991, 1/17 – Operation Desert Storm begins

2000 – Seventeen sailors tragically lose their lives after terrorists bomb the USS Cole

2003, 3/20 – Operation Iraqi Freedom begins

2011, 12/31 – Operation Iraqi Freedom ends

2012, 12/1 – The USS Enterprise is decommissioned after over 50 years of service.

ANIT Preparation

To achieve the best possible result on the ANIT, it is vital to constantly test your understanding of the sections you have covered. In addition to the practice test questions, you should consider engaging with the material in different ways. For example, you may wish to make a presentation from memory or try to construct a timeline of the Navy's history without any prompts.

The ANIT is also a section which can be aided by speaking with Navy personnel. If you know anyone who is currently serving in the Navy, be sure to talk with them about their understanding of and experience with the contents of the ANIT. Hearing about Naval history from a veteran, for example, can bring it to life in a way that merely reading it cannot hope to.

The ANIT is also a great opportunity to engage with real life media as much as possible. By viewing photographs and videos of Navy aircraft and ships, and thinking about them in terms of the material covered by the ANIT, you will increase your ability to apply abstract concepts, such as axes, to real life situations that you will encounter during the course of your Navy career.

Many people find it useful to study with others when preparing for the ANIT. This is due to the fact that some people are naturally more passionate and enthusiastic about some sections than others. For example, you may have a buddy who has a real passion for the way in which airports operate, while you may be more interested in the history of the Navy. By studying together and teaching each other about your area of interest and expertise, you are likely to benefit each other more than you could hope to studying alone.

ANIT Practice Test

1. When is the birthday of the Navy?

    A. October 13th 1775
    B. October 17th 1775
    C. October 13th 1773
    D. October 17th 1776

2. What color markings are used for taxiways?

    A. White
    B. Red
    C. Yellow
    D. Green

3. A large white X on a runway indicates

    A. The point where the pilot should land
    B. The runway is for helicopters only
    C. The runway is clear and a landing is permitted
    D. The runway is not in use

4. If a VASI shows all white

    A. The pilot is flying too low
    B. The pilot is flying too high
    C. The pilot is flying correctly
    D. A VASI cannot show all white

5. The highest classification of airspace in the USA is

    A. Class A
    B. Class G
    C. Class E
    D. Class B

6. The lateral axis of a plane runs

    A. From one wing of the plane to the other
    B. From the nose of the plane to the tail
    C. From the plane's highest point to its lowest point
    D. Diagonally from corner to corner

7. A ship's keel refers to

    A. Its captain
    B. Its deck
    C. Its major structural component
    D. Keel refers to planes, not ships

8. The closest layer of the atmosphere to the Earth's surface is the

    A. Stratosphere
    B. Exosphere
    C. Thermosphere
    D. Troposphere

9. Total drag consists of

    A. Vortex drag + Parasite drag
    B. Parasite drag + Form drag
    C. Vector drag + Induced drag
    D. Induced drag + Parasite drag

10. Operation Desert Storm began in

    A. 1992
    B. 1993
    C. 1991
    D. 1990

11. Yellow chevrons on a runway indicate

    A. The first point where a plane can land
    B. The taxiway
    C. Unsuitability for use unless in an emergency
    D. An area for takeoffs and not landings

12. A hold position sign is colored

    A. Red
    B. White
    C. Red and white
    D. Yellow

13. The area between the water level and base of a ship is called

   A. Draft
   B. Deck
   C. Keel
   D. Freeboard

14. A nautical mile is

   A. 6,067 ft
   B. 6,076 ft
   C. 7,067 ft
   D. 7,076 ft

15. Terrain association refers to

   A. Choosing the right vehicle for a mission
   B. Navigating using GPS
   C. Navigating using geographical features
   D. The suitability of a ship's materials for certain weather

16. The start of the landing portion of a runway is called the

   A. Displaced barrier
   B. Displaced threshold
   C. Threshold barrier
   D. Chevron limit

17. Cruisers are named with the following letters

   A. CB
   B. CF
   C. CA
   D. CG

18. The USS Enterprise served for

   A. Over 20 years
   B. Over 30 years
   C. Over 40 years
   D. Over 50 years

19. Omnidirectional lighting means

    A. Lighting pointing in the direction planes taxi
    B. Lighting pointing towards the main airport building
    C. Lighting that can be turned in any direction
    D. Lighting which lights up every direction at the same time

20. If two aircraft approach each other head on, they should

    A. Radio for emergency help
    B. Both give way to the right
    C. Both give way to the left
    D. Make an arrangement between pilots

ANIT Answer Key

1. A
2. C
3. D
4. B
5. A
6. A
7. C
8. D
9. D
10. C
11. C
12. C
13. A
14. B
15. C
16. B
17. D
18. D
19. D
20. B

Mechanical Comprehension Test (MCT)

MCT Purpose

The ASTB's Mechanical Comprehension Test, or MCT, is designed to test your understanding of both abstract and applied mechanical and physical concepts, which are relevant to Navy sailing and aviation. This involves both understanding pure formulas, such as the equation for pressure, as well as considering practical, applied ideas, such as the weight of different materials.

Aside from the Aviation and Nautical Information Test, the MCT is perhaps the most directly relevant to your future Naval career. Unlike more abstract sections such as the RCT, you will likely use the information and skills tested by the MCT throughout your day to day military career. You can therefore study with the motivation that the information you learn will be useful not only for the ASTB itself, but for your everyday working life in the future. Studying hard and acquiring knowledge will continue to benefit you far beyond the date of your ASTB.

Depending on your future role in the Navy, you will be required to work with incredibly complex machines and vehicles. Understanding the mechanical principles at work allows you to operate them in the most informed way possible, leading to a more optimum level of performance.

The MCT also demonstrates your ability to think in a technical, scientific way, and to apply the concepts of pure physics to a more practical context. This shows the Navy that you have the right mindset and understanding to go far in a technically demanding role.

MCT Contents

Center Of Gravity

The center of gravity of an object can be understood as the average location of the weight of an object. This is the point at which objects behave as if all of their mass is concentrated.

A ball is a good way of understanding the concept of center of gravity. If you throw a ball up in the air, it comes down directly. The center of gravity is its center. This is due to the fact that a ball is an even shape and therefore has a predictable center of gravity.

If you think about the human body, however, the center of gravity is not at the halfway point of a person's height. This is due to the fact that there is more mass above the halfway point than below it. The center of gravity of a person is therefore above their middle.

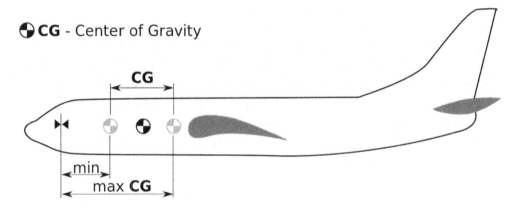

Torque

Torque is a force that measures the extent to which an object is caused to rotate by the forces acting on it. Objects rotate around an axis, known as the pivot point. The distance between the pivot point and the distance where the force acts is called the moment arm.

Torque = Force × perpendicular distance from the pivot

For example, a door rotates about its hinges while opening and closing. It can be seen that torque is directly proportional to force, and perpendicular distance from the pivot. If you think about the action of opening a door, you will realize that pushing the door closer to its hinge makes it more difficult to open the door, whereas pushing the door farther from the hinge makes it easier to open.

To consider another way in which torque impacts the real world, envision a crane. Due to the arm of the crane being a length away from the pivot point, counterweights are used in order to offset the torque, which prevents rotation from occurring. This is an illustration of how torque must be counterbalanced in order to achieve stability.

Friction

Friction is easy to envisage. Imagine pushing an object that is on the floor. It will not glide smoothly, instead, there will be a certain level of resistance from the floor. Or, picture jumping from a diving board at a swimming pool. The resistance of the air against your body is another type of friction. One of the benefits of friction is that, without it, objects would continue moving indefinitely until an outside force acted on them.

Static & Kinetic Friction

Static friction can be understood as the force acting between two things that are in contact with each other while not moving. If you picture a coffee cup sitting on a table, static friction occurs between the cup and the table which resists movement. Static friction only applies to objects at rest, as movement instead causes kinetic friction to apply.

In order to move an object, static friction must be overcome. Picture pushing the coffee cup resting on the table incredibly gently with your pinky finger. The cup will not move straight away. Instead, you must apply a certain amount of force before the cup moves. The instant that the coffee cup begins to move is an indication that a sufficient level of force has been exerted in order to overcome the static friction between the cup and the table.

Mathematically static and kinetic friction are given by:

Fs = μ_s × Normal Force

Fk = μ_k × Normal Force

where, μ is the coefficient of friction.

Kinetic friction only increases until a point. After a certain level of force has been exerted, motion happens at the same rate. Picture pushing a box along the floor. At first, you may move it slowly, before the motion increases as you apply more force. After a while, you will not see any increase in motion, as the kinetic friction has been minimized to the furthest point possible.

Energy

The law of conservation of energy is expressed as "energy can neither be created or destroyed, only changed from one form to another." A simple illustration is an electric kettle, which changes electrical energy into heat energy, for example. The energy isn't created, merely changed.

Energy is a scalar quantity with the SI unit of Joule, J and 1 J is equal to 1 Nm. Energy is also measured in foot-pounds force which can also be expressed as ft. lbf.

Potential Energy

Potential energy occurs when an object is in a certain position in relation to its default position. Consider this with the following two examples. When a bow, used to fire arrows, is slack, it contains no stored energy. However, when the bow's string is drawn back, it contains potential energy. Also, consider a heavy ball at rest on the floor. In its default position on the floor, the ball does not contain stored energy. However, if the ball is raised and held off the floor, then it contains stored potential energy.

Potential Energy = mass × acceleration due to gravity × height = mgh

Kinetic Energy

Any object in motion has kinetic energy, whether that movement happens to be vertical or horizontal.

$$\text{Kinetic Energy} = \frac{1}{2} \times \text{mass} \times (\text{velocity of the body})^2 = \frac{1}{2} mv^2$$

For example; in an ideal frictionless environment, consider an object is at rest at a certain height, and its potential energy (often represented by U) is equal to mgh. At this point, the object has full potential energy, and no kinetic energy. Next, the object is dropped. As it falls, its potential energy is converted into kinetic energy as the object moves through the air. Just before the object hits the ground, it has used all of its potential energy, and has only kinetic energy. Then, when the object hits the ground, its kinetic energy is converted into different forms of energy. This might take the form of heat or sound energy, for example.

To picture some other examples of energy conservation occurring, think about how the sun converts nuclear energy to various forms of electromagnetic energy, such as gamma, ultraviolet, and infrared, or how the human body is capable of converting chemical energy from food into mechanical energy required to move.

Work

Work is defined as the product of force and displacement. When a body is moved through a distance, the work done by the body is proportional to the force applied and the distance through which it is displaced. Mathematically:

Work done = Force × displacement

Work is measured in foot-pound force; ft. lbf. The SI unit of work is Joule or Nm.

In order to understand this idea through an example, think about an object which starts off at rest on the ground.

Example 1

The object is pushed and, as a result of the force applied to it, it moves. The movement in the same direction of the applied force is due to work.

Example 2

An object is lifted off the ground, going against the gravity acting downwardly upon it. As the force is moving the object upward, and the displacement (movement) of the object is upward, this is another example of work done.

Examples of Work Not Done

There are situations when, logically, you may expect work to occur, but, according to the laws of physics, it does not. Imagine you are pushing very hard against a wall, exerting a lot of force. Even though you may consider yourself to be "working," no work is done in the physics sense of the word due to the fact that no motion (displacement) is happening as a result of your force. Without force, and displacement in the same direction as the force, no work has happened.

Similarly, if a force acts upon an object, but the object does not move in the direction of the force applied to it, but due to some other force, then no work has occurred resulting from the initial force.

Power

Power is defined as the rate of work done. Mathematically:

$$Power = \frac{Work\ done}{Time\ Taken}$$

SI unit of power is Watt, symbol W, which is mathematically equal to J/s. Other units of power are horsepower and foot-pound per second or ft-lb/s.

1 horsepower = 550 ft-lb/s

1 horsepower = 746 J/s = 746 W

As the above equation and examples show, for power to be above zero, work must occur. Without work, there is no power. Picture yourself holding a heavy bag of flour stationary above the ground. There is no work, as there is no displacement, and therefore power is zero. This is the case even though effort is being exerted to hold the heavy bag of flour in place.

Scalars And Vectors

All physical quantities like length, time, mass, speed, velocity, force, etc., can be broadly classified into Scalars and Vectors.

Scalar

This is a measurement which has only a size (magnitude) but not a direction. For example, your mass as a human being is an example of a scalar. It has only size, but no direction.

Vector

Vectors are those physical quantities that have both magnitude (size) and direction. For example, two points X and Y are 10 m apart. The distance between the 2 points is 10 m, but if a person leaves point X and travels a distance of 10m toward the right, to reach point Y, the distance no longer remains a scalar quantity but becomes a vector quantity called "displacement."

The displacement made by the person is 10 m from X to Y. If the person returns to X from Y, the distance is still 10 m, but the displacement is -10 m from Y to X. In physics, the directions of vector quantities can be left, right, downward, upward, forward, and backward. Direction of vectors is determined by positive and negative signs. As shown in the above example, the displacement from X to Y was indicated by a positive symbol, whereas the displacement in the opposite direction, from Y to X, was indicated by a negative symbol.

Force And Newton's Laws Of Motion

Force is a vector quantity due to the fact that is has both a size (magnitude) and a direction. Force is measured in units of Newton, which are commonly shown by the symbol N. Force is also measured in pound-force, which is shown by the symbol lbf.

Newton's 1st Law of Motion

The Law of Inertia is another name that Newton's 1st Law of Motion is known by. Inertia is the force that resists motion within a body. The law states that "until an external force acts on an object, the object's velocity will remain constant."

This applies both to the case of an object at rest, which is bound to remain at rest until something acts on it, and also to an object in motion, which will remain in motion until acted upon. So why does a ball that is rolling not continue to roll? Due to outside forces acting on it, such as friction. Without the presence of such outside forces, the ball would never stop moving!

Newton's 2nd Law of Motion

This law states the principle that in order to stop or move an object, the force required to do so is directly in proportion to the mass of the object. For example, if an object is heavier, it requires more force to either make it move or stop it moving, than if the object was lighter, and vice versa. Think about a small toy car rolling down a hill next to a full-size lorry. It would require very little force to stop the toy car from moving, whereas stopping the lorry would require a great deal more force.

This is Newton's 2nd Law of Motion. Mathematically, the law is:

Force = Mass of the body × Acceleration on the body

Acceleration can be understood as the rate of change.

Newton's 3rd Law of Motion

Newton's 3rd Law of Motion states that "for every action, there is an equal and opposite reaction." Picture firing a gun. The gun exerts force on the bullet, but the bullet also exerts a force in reaction, back against the gun, causing the gun to recoil as a result. Another example is when you sit on a chair; you are exerting a force downward on the chair, but the chair is exerting a force upward on you. This latter example is a case of static equilibrium.

Static equilibrium contrasts with dynamic equilibrium. To envision dynamic equilibrium, imagine a man on a skateboard rolling down a hill towards another man, who is standing still. If the two collide, then they exert an equal and opposite force against each other. This causes the man on the skateboard to stop moving and be knocked off his board, while it causes the man standing still to not be at rest, and go flying in the direction of the force exerted on him by the man rolling down the hill.

Centripetal And Centrifugal Forces

In order to understand these two forces, picture a ball tied to a post by a rope, like a tetherball. When the ball moves around the post in a circular path, the centripetal force is the force acting through the rope towards the center, allowing for the circular motion. The centrifugal force acts in opposition to this centripetal force, which maintains the tension found in the rope.

Newton's Law Of Gravitation And Weight

According to Newton's Law of Gravitation, every object in existence is attracted to every other object by a force directly proportional to their masses and inversely proportional to the square of the distance between them. Mathematically the force between two bodies is given by:

$$Force = \frac{G \; x \; mass \; of \; body \; 1 \; x \; mass \; of \; body \; 2}{Distance \; between \; the \; bodies \; ^2}$$

where, G is the constant of proportionality and is equal to 6.674×10^{-11} Nm^2/kg^2.

Gravity

According to the Law of Gravitation, the Earth exerts a pull on every object that is on Earth. This can be easily observed due to the difference in mass between the Earth and everything else on it. For example, if you think of a bowling ball and the Earth, the concept becomes clear. A bowling ball's mass is far, far less than that of the Earth, and the distance between the ball and the center of the Earth is equal to the radius of the Earth. If the bowling ball is dropped, it is pulled downward, in the direction of the Earth's center.

By substituting the Mass of the earth = 6×10^{24} kg, value of G and the radius of the earth = 6.4×10^6 m, the force or pull of earth can be calculated as 9.78 N $\approx$ 9.8 N. This is the constant force of attraction of our planet on each kilogram of matter. Acceleration due to gravity is equal to 9.8 m/s^2.

Consider the following formulas:

Force = mass × acceleration

Weight = mass × acceleration due to gravity

The SI unit of mass is kilograms and weight is Newton. Weight is a vector quantity, as it has a direction, and that direction is toward the center of the Earth. Due to the fact that all objects experience the same pull from the Earth, in a frictionless environment, every object would move towards the Earth at the same rate.

Mass vs Weight

While mass remains fixed at all times, the value for weight changes due to the difference in acceleration resulting from gravity. To illustrate this concept, picture a man walking on Earth, and the same man walking on the moon. Although the person has the same mass in either scenario, the weight of the person changes. We weigh a lot more on Earth, and a lot less on the moon, due to the difference in the strength of gravity.

Fluids And Hydraulics

Fluids

A fluid can be understood as anything that is able to flow while not being able to be compressed. Liquids and pressurized gas are the two most common examples of fluid. A use of fluid within the realm of physics and mechanics is to transmit force over a greater distance than would be possible with a mechanical system.

Pressure

Pressure is stated as force divided by area, and is measured in Pascals, expressed by the symbol Pa, pounds per square inch, expressed as psi, Newton's per meter squared, expressed as N/m^2, or inches of mercury (inHg). When pressure is applied to a liquid, the pressure acts equally on every point of the fluid.

Hydraulic pressure transmission

In a basic hydraulic system, pressure applied on the input piston is transmitted to the output piston by the fluid present in between them. Mathematically:

Input pressure = Output pressure

$$\left(\frac{Force}{Area}\right)_{Input} = \left(\frac{Force}{Area}\right)_{Output}$$

Mechanical advantage is given by:

Mechanical advantage $= \dfrac{Area\ of\ the\ output\ piston}{Area\ of\ the\ input\ piston}$

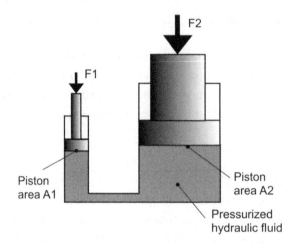

This mechanical advantage comes at a cost of distance moved by the piston. For example, a mechanical advantage of 2 means that the area of the output piston is double the area of the input piston, but it moves ½ the distance moved by the input piston.

Simple & Compound Machines

We can understand the mechanical advantage of a simple machine by using the following formula:

Mechanical advantage $= \dfrac{Output\ Force}{Input\ Force}$

It is important to note that simple machines do not actually generate power. Instead, they simply transfer or multiply power.

Let's look at some of the most common types of simple machines and the ways they work.

Levers

A level consists of three mechanical components – its input arm, its fulcrum, and its output arm.

Levers are categorized as being of one of three separate types, known as "classes." We'll now look at all three classes of lever to understand their uses, limitations, and ways of working.

First class levers

To picture a first class lever, envision a central fulcrum with input and output arms on either side. Input force is applied perpendicular to the input arm. This creates torque around the fulcrum. The fulcrum transfers this torque to the output arm. A seesaw works in this way, with the input arm being the left side of the seesaw, the fulcrum being the center point on which the seesaw rests, and the output arm being the right hand side of the seesaw.

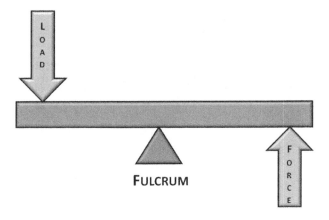

Second class levers

A second class lever has its output force between the input force and the fulcrum, such as in the case of a wheelbarrow, where the fulcrum is the middle of the wheel. When a large weight is put near to the fulcrum, it is possible to lift them with less effort than would usually be required due to the position of the fulcrum relative to the input point. A second class lever has a mechanical advantage which exceeds 1.

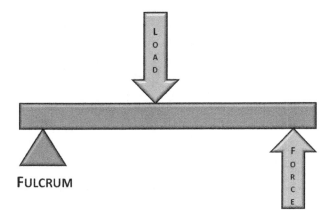

Third class levers

A third class lever can be pictured by thinking about an input force which is between the fulcrum and the output force. The human forearm is a good way to understand a third class lever. In the case of the forearm, the elbow joint acts as the fulcrum, the bicep muscle acts as the input force, and the swinging of the hand is the output force.

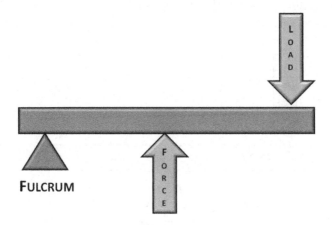

Inclined Planes

Inclined planes are a simple machine which have a slope at an angle to the ground, like a ramp. The advantage of using an inclined plane is that it allows an object to be moved upward along the length of the plane with less force than would be needed to lift the object vertically, requiring gravity to be overcome.

The mechanical advantage of an inclined plane is given by:

$$\text{Mechanical advantage} = \frac{Length\ of\ the\ inclined\ plane}{Height\ of\ the\ plane}$$

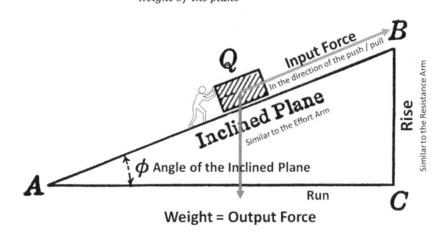

According to the formula, the longer the length of the ramp the greater the mechanical advantage. However, it is not feasible to make ramps with very long lengths. This is due to the fact that the weight of an object exerts a downward force on the ramp. Think about two sticks, one short and one long. The longer stick is far easier to snap. This is the same concept with an inclined plane. The longer it is, the more susceptible it is to breaking.

Screw

If you think about what a screw actually is, you will realize it consists of an inclined plane, like a ramp, running around the center of the screw's circumference, kind of like a spiral ramp. The distance between the threads of the screw is known as the pitch. The pitch is equal to the distance travelled by the screw after one full rotation.

The following formula shows the mechanical advantage of the screw. R is the moment arm and P is the pitch.

$$\frac{2\pi R}{P}$$

Wedges

If you think about a wedge, it consists of two inclined planes working in conjunction. Picture a knife, for example. If the knife is sharp, its cutting edge has a greater slope than a blunter knife. We can understand the mechanical advantage of an inclined plane with the following formula:

Mechanical advantage of wedge $= \dfrac{Length\ of\ Wedge}{Thickness\ across\ the\ Wedge}$

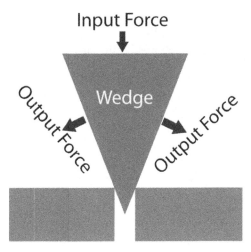

The longer a wedge is, and the thinner it is, the greater the mechanical advantage.

Pulleys

Tension in a string

Anything like a rope, cord, thread, or string has the force of tension when pulled at both ends. The tension is equal across the length of the rope. If a push force is applied, then no tension occurs. Resistance only happens in the case of a pull. This understanding is important for the following section.

Pulley and Wheel system

The pulley makes use of a rope being passed over a wheel and axle. The rope is pulled and the tension is transmitted through the entire rope equally, as described above. The difference here is that the wheel is able to alter the direction of the rope's tension. If you picture a frictionless environment, all of the input force (generated by the pull on the rope) is transmitted through the rope and into output. This would result in a mechanical advantage for this pulley system of 1.

$$\text{Mechanical advantage of pulley} = \frac{Input\ Force}{Output\ Force}$$

To increase the mechanical advantage here, it is necessary to use a number of different segments working in unison. In such a situation, the following applies:

Mechanical advantage of block and tackle = Number of cord segments

The block and tackle arrangement increases the mechanical advantage of the pulley system at the cost of distance moved by the output load.

Wheel and Axle

Wheel and axle form a type of simple machine, attached together coaxially. Their rotations are about their centers. The mechanical advantage is given by:

$$\text{Mechanical advantage} = \frac{Radius\ of\ Wheel}{Radius\ of\ Axle}$$

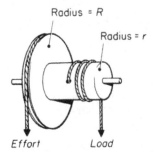

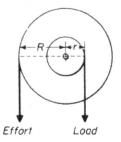

In some cases, a single axle can be used to rotate two wheels of different sizes. In such cases, the mechanical advantage is given by:

$$\text{Mechanical advantage} = \frac{Radius\ of\ Input\ Wheel}{Radius\ of\ Output\ Wheel}$$

This mechanical advantage is generated by the fact that the input and output torques are equal to one another. Picture the following: if a system such as this has a mechanical advantage of 2, then the input wheel would have to have a radius twice that of the output wheel. However, the output belt would travel one half of the distance in comparison to the input belt.

Gears

Gears are a way of transferring torque and rotation over a larger distance than would otherwise be possible. This is done by coupling wheels together with belts and chains.

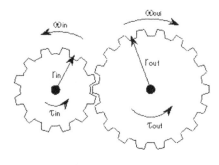

$$\text{Mechanical advantage of gear} = \frac{1}{Mechanical\ Advantage\ of\ Wheel\ and\ Axle}$$

Gears feature interlocking wheels where the direction of rotation for the output wheel is the opposite of the direction of rotation for the input wheel.

Picture a gear system where the mechanical advantage is 2. This would stem from the output gear being double the radius if the input gear. This would require the input gear to be rotated twice in order to rotate the output gear once. If the input gear is smaller than the output gear, then torque is multiplied whereas speed is reduced. If the input gear is bigger than the output gear, then the torque is reduced and the speed is increased.

Electrical Theory

The most important principle in Electrical Theory is Ohm's Law, expressed as $V = IR$, or Voltage = Current × Resistance.

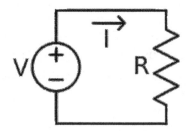

Voltage is a measurement of the unit charge required to move between two points.

Current is measured in Amperes, and measures the flow of charge in a circuit. Two types of current exist. Direct current, commonly referred to as DC, flows in one direction with a constant voltage polarity. Alternating current, or AC, alternates its direction and voltage polarity.

Resistance is measured in Ohms and measures the amount of current repulsion in a circuit.

Electrical Devices

Ammeter – A device used to measure current in Amperes (A)

Voltmeter – A device used to measure voltage in Volts (V)

Multimeter – Also known as a VOM (Volt-Ohm-Milliammeter), a single device able to measure voltage, current, and resistance

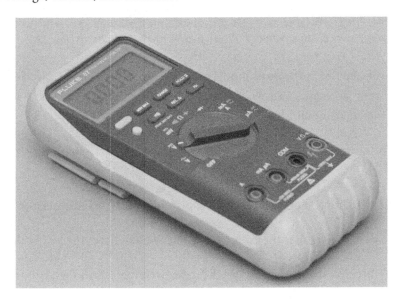

Four Stroke Engine

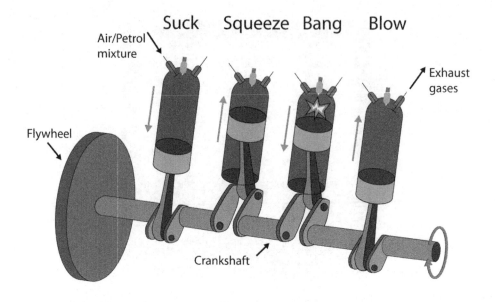

1. Suck - Induction Stroke - Air/Petrol mixture drawn in.
2. Squeeze - Compression Stroke - Valves close and piston moves up.
3. Bang - Power Stroke - Electric spark from spark plug ignites mixture.
4. Blow - Exhaust Stroke - Piston moves up pushing gases out.

The four stroke engine is the most modern engine type in the modern world, powering the majority of vehicles. As seen in the following diagram, the four stroke cycle consists of intake, compression, ignition, and exhaust.

Intake – The downward movement of the piston draws in a fresh mixture of vaporized air and fuel.

Compression – The rising movement of the piston compresses the fuel and air vapor.

Power – A spark plug ignites the compressed fuel, which drives the piston downward.

Exhaust – The exhaust valve opens and the exhausted fuel leaves the cylinder.

MCT Preparation

Of all the sections of the ASTB, the MCT contains some of the densest and most technical information of the entire test. It is therefore vital to engage with it repeatedly, to test your understanding and to ensure that you have retained your comprehension of anything you covered previously.

In order to approach the MCT in the most balanced and methodical way possible, you should first determine how much time you can allocate to this section of the ASTB. Then, divide this total time up between the number of topics you wish to cover. This guards against the problem of spending too much time on any one section, resulting in gaps in your knowledge.

Often, due to the technical nature of the concepts found in the MCT, reading and answering questions is not enough to gain the fullest understanding. Many people find it useful to engage with the material in other ways, such as by watching YouTube videos and drawing out diagrams in order to illustrate the mechanical principles tested.

Your ability to achieve a high score on the MCT portion of the ASTB effectively comes down to two factors: your understanding and your application. To improve your understanding, you may wish to use flashcards to make complex, intricate concepts more manageable. For example, rather than considering the topic of Ohm's law as a unified whole, you could use flashcards to test your understanding of its individual aspects, such as what V refers to, what IR are equal to, and so forth.

To test your application of the ideas, you may wish to write out a list of formulas and diagrams with sections missing. For example, you could draw a diagram of a simple machine with a section missing, or an equation with part of the solution missing. Then, at a later time, come back to these incomplete diagrams and equations and use them to test what you can recall. This will help to ensure that you don't just acquire abstract knowledge, but that you are also able to apply it to the type of problems you will encounter on the MCT.

MCT Practice Test

1. Torque causes

    A. Rotation
    B. Lift
    C. Thrust
    D. Mass

2. According to Newton's 2nd Law, force = ?

    A. Acceleration × Torque
    B. Torque × Weight
    C. Mass × Lift
    D. Mass × Acceleration

3. A first class lever has

    A. No fulcrum
    B. A fulcrum between the input and output arms
    C. A fulcrum to the right of the input and output arms
    D. A fulcrum to the left of the input and output arms

4. The four stages of a four stroke engine cycle are

    A. Intake, Compression, Generation, Exhaust
    B. Input, Compression, Power, Exit
    C. Input, Compression, Power, Exhaust
    D. Intake, Compression, Power, Exhaust

5. Ohm's Law can be expressed through the formula

    A. $V = IR$
    B. $P = IR$
    C. $V = IS$
    D. $P = IN$

6. A multimeter is also known as a

    A. VIM
    B. VAM
    C. VOM
    D. VEM

7. Mechanical advantage is determined by

    A. Output Force × Input Force
    B. Input Force + Output Force
    C. Output Force / Input Force
    D. Output Force – Input Force

8. A ball's center of gravity is

    A. At its top
    B. Directly in its center
    C. At its lowest point
    D. It depends on the ball

9. Kinetic friction increases

    A. Up until a point
    B. Indefinitely
    C. Kinetic friction does not increase
    D. Kinetic friction exists but can't be quantified

10. To move an object, you must overcome

    A. Static Friction
    B. Torque
    C. Lift
    D. Voltage

11. Work done =

    A. Force × Mass
    B. Force / Mass
    C. Force / Displacement
    D. Force × Displacement

12. Another name for Newton's First Law is

    A. The Law of Motion
    B. The Law of Inertia
    C. The Law of Energy
    D. The Law of Momentum

12. When considering mass and weight

   A. Both mass and weight are fixed
   B. Neither mass and weight are fixed
   C. Mass is fixed but weight varies
   D. It depends on the situation

14. Scalars have

   A. Magnitude but not direction
   B. Direction but not magnitude
   C. Both direction and magnitude
   D. Neither direction or magnitude

15. The distance between the threads of a screw is known as the

   A. Plane
   B. Ridge
   C. Pitch
   D. Jump

16. A block and tackle is used to

   A. Counter torque
   B. Increase mechanical advantage
   C. Decrease lift
   D. Increase structural integrity

17. A basic hydraulic system transmits pressure using

   A. An input piston, an output piston, and fluid
   B. An input piston, compressed air, and an output valve
   C. An input piston, compressed air, and an output piston
   D. An input gear, compressed fluid, and an output piston

18. How many classes of lever are there?

   A. 1
   B. 2
   C. 3
   D. 4

19. A screw makes use of which simple machine?

    A. Pulley
    B. Gear
    C. Wedge
    D. Inclined plane

20. Gears transfer

    A. Lift
    B. Thrust
    C. Weight
    D. Torque

MCT Answer Key

1. A
2. D
3. B
4. D
5. A
6. C
7. C
8. B
9. A
10. A
11. D
12. B
13. C
14. A
15. C
16. B
17. A
18. C
19. D
20. D

ASTB Conclusion

The ASTB Study Guide is now complete.

By this stage, you should be able to answer affirmatively to the following statements:

1. I am familiar with the layout and structure of the ASTB Test.
2. I have studied the material for each section of the ASTB.
3. I have repeatedly taken practice tests.
4. I know which sections I am stronger on and weaker on.
5. I have a plan in place to address my weak points.

One of the keys to success on the ASTB is to use whatever time you have to prepare for the test efficiently.

Be sure to have a structured plan allowing you to address any areas of weakness and to maintain your existing knowledge.

It is far better to space out your learning and testing over a period of time, rather than trying to cram. Digesting knowledge in small amounts, with proper periods of rest, is a key to retaining information.

Also, don't overlook the administrative aspects of the ASTB due to covering the actual test material. Be sure to register at your desired test location, remember your testing date and time, and have a concrete plan in place to travel to the test center. The ASTB is too important to make a simple but crucial mistake in this area.

Finally, good luck. We wish you every success in your ASTB test and your future Naval career.

Useful External ASTB Resources

Navy Medicine's answers to the most commonly asked ASTB questions
www.med.navy.mil/sites/nmotc/nami/Pages/ASTBFrequentlyAskedQuestions.aspx

Official site dedicated to Naval history
www.history.navy.mil

An MIT website explaining the basic physics of flight
web.mit.edu/16.00/www/aec/flight.html

A list of free flight simulators (helpful for the PBM section of the ASTB)
http://www.digitaltrends.com/gaming/best-free-flight-simulators/

A YouTube channel showing both practical and theoretical aspects of airplane flight
www.youtube.com/user/profpilotcouk/videos

A YouTube channel with in-depth documentaries about Naval History and various craft
www.youtube.com/user/WarsChannel10/videos

Made in the USA
Coppell, TX
20 October 2020